2004

SELF-HELP
SELF-LOVE
SELF-DISCOVERY
SELF-PERCEPTION

YCARP LEAHCIMRAC

PAGE PUBLISHING
Conneaut Lake, PA

First originally published by Page Publishing 2024

Warning: some poems may contain disturbing
words. Readers' discretion is advised.

ISBN 979-8-89315-217-3 (pbk)
ISBN 979-8-89315-231-9 (digital)

Printed in the United States of America

INTRODUCTION

Majority of children born into the world are born by accident. I was born in 2004. The worst part is, I didn't even have a chance to breathe air nor was given a chance to be loved. No hate to my dad, but it still hurts to know you came to see if I had died after my mom had suffered through giving me life. Now look at me.

Communication has never been a strong taste for me until I got into poetry. So I welcome you to a journey that spans from childhood to adolescence in my life, a narrative woven with threads of choices, family, and the unseen cries for help. This poetry book is a testament to my experiences, a chronicle of the formative years that have shaped me. It delves into the complexities of relationships, the impact they have had on my psyche, and how they have molded my decisions.

It's an exploration of the silent battles we fight, I fought, and the hurt that often goes unnoticed by those around us. It's a call to the world to look beyond the surface and to understand the depth of our emotions.

This is not just a book; it's a piece of my soul. These were my secrets, a glimpse into my world. As you turn the pages, I hope you find a piece of yourself within these lines, a resonance with your own experiences while trying to understand mine.

MOMMY AND DADDY

There's no turning back, moving forward but facing resistance.
As I stay awake, I fail to sleep, feeling as I squeal.
Mommy and Daddy, it starts with you, not me.
I felt abandoned and confused. It's hard to see.
I love you both, though hate sometimes brews as I blame you for the hurt, mistakes, and blues that happened to me.
Neither of you knew the pain I endured.
Daddy, you made me felt lonely and unloved for sure,
Because of you, I don't know when a love from a man is actually true.
And to my mother, although you never knew, you took away my voice when I needed you too.
I had to realize pain lingers no matter how.
As I am grateful for you, I struggle to see why gratitude is due.
I felt as though you both weren't grateful to have me, not happy it seems.
You've adopted, tolerated, love only happened in my dreams.
Mom and Dad, I'm tired of living the life you planned for me.
Searching for my own path to truly understand this.
I long to be me and actually feel loved by you, authentically true, not the version of me that was shaped by you two.

FILL MY VOID

In the figure of my life, there's a void that was never built.
A father's love, a guiding hand, that was never quite there.
Like a lighthouse in the storm, my memories with you flicker, in and
out when I try to think of you some more.
A love that was never formed felt like it got lost in the snow.
Your absence echoed loudly, in the silence of my heart as I thought
of our bond, it feels like shadows, dancing in the night but I'm
always alone.
I say I love you often, words I whisper knowing they are not entirely
true.
I yearned for your presence even though I've learned to navigate life's
water, with a compass all on my own.
And while I miss you, Father, in ways you'll never know,
I've learned to love the person that your absence made me to be a lot
more.

I LOVE AND HATE YOU, MY DEAR

My sister, my guide, enduring every tide.
In your love and care, I take pride in you even when you're not here.
    Although we share a pain you can't remember.
Our tears are not just hormones, they're deeper than they may seem.
    In our shared memories, love do appears,
I show you hate, but it's all fake.
Yet in my heart, a yearning grows, not only for me but for you when
    I'm not there.
A wish from freedom, as the river flows.
Not from your love, so deep and pure, although you caused me so
    much pain.
I cherish you, my sister dear, but I long to venture far and near.
I don't want to be with you anymore.
No more us, no more we, no more love,
I wish to be free from your curse.
It's time for you to allow me to feel free and roam freely, as my love
    for you will never wane, even as I seek my own lane.

SHE'S BACK

Thought I ran far away she'll never be able to catch me.
As I began to feel better, there's always that one reminder of why I
don't deserve to feel accustomed.
Constantly blaming myself it felt like an unknown illness no doctor
can cure.
I yearned for that cure.
"You don't know what you feel, you're just a child," but I did know.
As she asked me if I wanted to hide or seek, I hid.
I let her grab me and controlled me and I felt okay with it, I accepted
it.
Deep down inside I always knew she'll always hold me as I believed
I was free.
With her I walked through the door, allowing all that negative to be
a part of me because with it, I could do anything not letting no
one hurt me.
I let her be my shield I couldn't.
I don't feel so empty, but I was still angry.

BE BY MY SIDE

Sometimes, I wonder if depression is something people choose to be in.

Living with a mom who only believed that depression is the only cause if you don't have everything, you should be happy.

Waking up to the same routine, I felt like I was living in a maze. I've forgiven but never seem to forget.

I endured the burden from my past so curl, it made me unkind.

My shadows were like an ogre sneaking in at night, leaving me hypnagogic. I felt I was never a warrior, couldn't keep up in a fight.

Even after being abused and forsaken allowing my monsters to dim my light, I held on to that desire to fight.

Having to live every day in a world awfully cold.

I know my journey to be free and live for me would be vast, but I am ready to be healed and remodeled from my past.

Walking into a path unclear, although it took me a while, I still grew to be resilient.

Here's to me raising from below.

Turning my pain into strength

My fear into devotion

All because I became determined to be healed and remodel my past for me.

ARE YOU OKAY?

In today's world, why is seeing someone unhappy okay to ignore?
Why is it okay to witness someone standing alone, when a simple question would have made a difference?
"Are you okay?"
A suspicion that has the potential to change their day and alter their emotions,
To make them realize at that moment as they do not themselves that someone out there truly cares.
But sometimes, we choose to mind our own business, and that's fair.
Yet is it fair that by choosing to stay silent, someone had to lose their life the next day?
Therefore, I want to say loud and clear, to hell with it,
I'm going to be that person who asks that question,
I'm going to be that person who has a smile on my face even if it feels meaningless.
My smile is a reminder that I have the firmness to overcome any bad day and be able to make another person smile.

NOTICE ME

I could remember waking up consumed by hate, building anger day
    by day, only to forget the reason why.
Deep down, I didn't want to be miserable, for it stole away my smile.
I felt as blank as night,
Empty as a desert with no oasis in sight,
And My crown lost its shine,
As my heart fell as far as the apple from the tree.
No matter how much I scrubbed, washed, and rinsed
I still felt as if I had played in a mud bath filled with nothing but
    negativity and hate.
The dirt of all that hate still clung to me.
Because of that hate, it overshadowed any happiness I sought.
I had to lose myself to find myself.
So yes,
Even with new pain, I will smile.
Even as I take a step forward and life pushes me back, I will smile.
Because as I smile, I understand that it's okay to stumble when being
    on the path to happiness.

BLAME ME

I've been carrying a burden in my heart for as long as I can remember.
My spirit feels weighed down,
It's time to pray.
Oh, Lord, as I'm on my knees, hear my voice as I speak your name.
Hear my pain, notice my tears, and heal my heartache as I talk to you
of the one I miss the most.
Allow me to talk to him, allow me to feel his presence as I call out
his name.
Grandfather, my everything, taken away without a sound.
His voice, his smile, his honest remarks
I can't comprehend how much I need that so much.
I felt alone, lost in despair.
You were my grandfather but acted more as a father that I needed
when I'm scared.
I lost both that day, I lost you that day.
I wanted to be blamed, it's all unfair
Your absence, a void, too great to fill,
I had to learn to live without that day.
Having to remember your love for me is like a guiding star, shining
on me, from afar every day.
Life got tough, too hard to bear.
It should've been me, not you, that day.
I know life's always going to be unfair.
So I'll live for you, as if you are here, you're never forgotten because I
know you'll always be here.

ONE STEP AWAY FROM MY FEAR

Fear is but a threat, lurking in my life.
Here's a word of advice that that keeps me going throughout my life,
Fear may attempt to cage us, to hold control of our life,
But remember, fear is just an ultimatum, waiting to be met.
I've faced it, fought it, and won.
So to my next challenge, bring it on, do your worst,
Because what can be worse to know I've allowed my fears to shake
    me to defeat.
My fears do not cage me as I discover it's but the key.
And to you my fears, I refuse to hide when I've gotten the key to
    fight.

MY REFLECTIONS

You see the title I've chosen for my poem, it's "My Reflections," not just "My Reflection" alone.
Within me, many personalities reside, as I allow them to be free, many others would confide.
I became afraid to gaze into the mirror, as I got used to it becoming shattered. My eyes are too big or small, my ears are just too small.
My nose, it seems big, never small, and my lips I wished were small.
I often find myself closing my eyes, just standing there, to shield myself from the reflections I can't bear.
As they talk to me, reminding me of what I wish wasn't there,
A reminder of an image I can't replace nor escape.
The word *attractive* carries a weight I despise,
It hinders me from seeing my inner glow, my prize I wish this wasn't a lie.
I must admit, each reflection breeds negativity I try to escape.
I lived with a shadow of self-disgrace that I can't commit.
I lived with so much self-hate I carried deep inside,
But I channel that hate into motivation one day.
As it guided me to the path I needed to grow, each day I strived as I found my light that was once dim by my lies.

LOOK INTO MY EYES

My eyes, windows to my soul's inner quest, seeking truths, desires,
    and what's truly best.
If you look closer and notice they hold the stories of my hidden pain
    yet yearn for happiness, my own domain.
In darkness, I can easily hide my pain.
But no need to hide when they don't even notice my aches.
I deserve to feel bright, no longer reliant on another's touch,
I found solace within, I can't believe I'm saying this.
But I love myself so much.
Unveiling the path to my own serenity, through sadness, hurt, and
    the lingering shade, I'll find my way to happiness, unswayed.
So, yes, my eyes will shine with resilience and grace, I will reflect the
    journeys toward my own embrace.
I'll find my way to see more no matter how far the view is afar.

MY FRIENDS

Finally, a weightlifter.
I'm relieved, I beg for this freedom, it's liberation, I can make a new
    chapter.
A chance to prove, to show I don't need you, I never did.
I was caught in the echoes of their thoughts, their expectations for
    me.
They wanted me to feel dependent.
More so on them.
I became inseparable, and the constant presence was stifling, a bore.
Now, they're gone, my smile is genuine and can be seen more, no
    more need for pretense.
The irony is I found joy in my own company, as I embraced solitude.

CHEERING YOU ON, BUT I WON'T CALL YOU A FRIEND

Know my faith in you won't bend,
So let me speak as my words flow as you remember this till the end.
I'll be cheering you on, even though I won't call you a friend.
Thinking of you as I walked, I felt out of step.
Promises made, promises kept, but not on your end. Your words,
    once sweet, now seem so hollow.
I'm so unkept.
As I think of seeing you,
I felt as if it was a bitter pill hard to swallow.
Not even water can clinch my struggles.
I felt left out, pushed aside,
In the shadow of your pride.
In the end, it's clear to see I too had made a mistake.
Yes, I'm known to lose my cool and push you aside too.
As you insisted it'll be all right, of course that was a lie.
So to my friend, my last words to you I said before and I will again,
    "I'll be cheering you on, even though I won't call you a friend."

These pieces are more than just words; they're raw, unfiltered journeys through my childhood I'm ready to release. They encapsulate the pain, struggle, and resilience that shaped me into the person I am working on today. They might be difficult to hear but harder to tell, but they're my truths. And from this day forward, I believe in the power of sharing our truths no matter how painful they might be, allowing our voice to be heard and being able to feel free.

I know the ending is a little corny, but let's get to reading shall we?

WANT THE TRUTH?

I'm struggling, can't breathe, it's like someone's choking me.
Now life's getting harder and harder bringing me down, I can tell
soon I'll fall.
I allowed curiosity to win as I looked at my arm, wondering, should
I? What's wrong with me?
I solved the problem with self-sabotage.
Living in the shadows of having to be myself not knowing who I am
yet.
Daddy says, "Never be like your mom,"
But all I hear is, "You are just like your mom."
Seeking consolation as I weep made me feel weak.
Turning for hardware to numb the feeling that couldn't be helped
by me.
I wished I knew real healing comes from love that's real.
Now I know it took me this long to heal 'cause I never had the love I
needed that felt real to heal.

THE FEELING STILL LINGERS

I forgive, but never seemed to forget.
Though I can't recall your name, your presence still lingers as I try to
    remember your face.
How do they sleep knowing the pain they've caused?
A question I asked myself day by day because of my thoughts.
No one heard as I cried myself to sleep every night.
No one listened, my voice silenced, trapped within each bite.
The pain became too painful to utter, and I began to blame myself.
"Was it my fault?" Could have never been.
I was young, naive, unaware of the harm inflicted upon me.
I knew it was wrong, the feeling never felt right to me.
Those days remain etched in my memory, different faces, different
    places, why me?
Strangers and acquaintances, I never trusted, you all should be grown
    now, perhaps have forgotten your deeds, but I sure haven't.
Abandoned house where hopelessness consumed us, as we unknow-
    ingly became the sacrifice for his soul.
You were meant to protect us, but instead, you traded us.
Our innocence is gone the day you baited us.
Young as you were, you knew the plan, the harm you inflicted upon
    us.
One by one, we fell into the abyss.
One by one, he carried out his sinful deeds as planned.
We watched in shock, speechless, as we left with no ice cream.
Your attempts to take away my innocence, you all have won.

NEXT CHAPTER

It's finally over, a chapter now closed, but the journey ahead, still
unknown and exposed.

I've told myself you're free, although deep down I know, there's a
lingering feeling, a part that won't let go.

As I ask myself constantly, "When will this tangled confusion come
to an end?"

I find myself stuck, questioning what comes next, in this grand
illusion,

I keep feeling I just don't belong.

I questioned myself and the choices I've made as I reminded myself
of at least three choices that "I made."

No regrets, just lessons learned along the way.

Each step forward, another shade of gray.

My future feels distant in thoughts as I feel I don't deserve any good
that comes to me.

Self-sabotage has always been my harmful game.

I never enjoyed it as I played, even as I felt myself ready to roll the
next dice.

I knew I was hurting myself, only causing more pain.

As I kept playing my game, I got bored and just wanted it to stop
causing pain.

Self-improvement is what I truly desire, but right now, I'm not happy,
I'm feeling tired.

It's time to decide, to find my own way, but lost in the sands of time,
I sway.

WHY WON'T I JUST FORGET

In the quiet corners of my mind, I long to forget.
Memories that haunt, leaving me with regrets I long to forget.
Why won't I just forget?
I desire freedom, a life that's all mine.
As I pray and beg for my god to erase, to wipe my slate clean,
To be able to unseen and feel the scene.
Leaving only what's in my present, and to be free at last.
But bitterly, the mind is a stubborn critter, refusing to let go.
Yet although I know, in forgetting, we lose the lessons learned, the
    growth, the strength, the bridges burned.
I pray to not forget but find peace, in the chaos of my memories,
    finding that release within me.

MY VOICE WILL BE HEARD

Hear my voice as I release my pain. Victim they say, fighter I say.
Victim no more, hear my empowering calls as I say their names. A struggle I've battled, a fight, a battle within.
Yet the strongest steel I've ever been.
Yes, tears will fall, like the heaviest rain, but remember, dear friends, there's no rainbow without a little rain.
Each challenge I've faced, every hardship I've met.
Never deserve the hurt that I've felt, though the past may have scarred, and memories sting,
I'm not just a victim, I'm a survivor with wings. My strength is my shield
So to survive to another when in the face of adversity, let your courage be your pride.
You're not only a victim, you're so much more within.

SPEAK YOUR TRUTHS

I'll speak my truths, I will be heard,
Refused to be silent, like a cage bird.
Though it took time to be known, my voice is the strongest weapon
that I know.
In a world so tall, full of noises, and voices so loud, I'm finally tall
enough and feeling strong.
Don't let your past hold you back, let them range as you speak your
truth, even when it's hard to say.
You never know who might care, speak your truths even when you're
scared, or caught off guard because your story is always worth
the share.
So speak your truth, let it ring clear, for it's your truth that people
need to hear.

THE PAST IS HARD TO DIGEST

After all the hurt and painful memories I had to deal with, I became
a warrior, ready for any fight.
No more monsters lurking in the night.
After being abused and neglected, I found my light.
Holding onto hope with all my might, I became my own knight.
No support, no help, the world seemed so cold,
Yet within my spirit, a fire so bold.
I dream of a future, free from my past,
Where love and kindness no hurt would find me at last.
My journey was indeed a great sorrow, more reasons I was deter-
mined to heal and recast.
You can too.
My life seemed hard, every new path seemed more uncleared,
Yet I walked through them despite the fear of failing.
For I knew my strength was near, in my heart my power to do more
was clear.
I am a teen, my life is hard,
Yet I am a poet, my soul a bard. My past was my teacher.
It taught me how to rise from below and turned my pain into strength.
Use me as a testament to what you're capable of,
When we face our fears, and give ourselves a loving shove.

ARE WE HEALED?

Words don't have to be a lot to mean a lot.
There are days we think we've forgotten, yet it's all just a thought.
One moment we're as joyful as a child, the next as grumpy as an ogre
    sought.
Our feelings, they flutter in disorder,
Wishing it all could just be over.
But let me keep this brief, I know the desire for it to be over,
Yet if I can keep going, keep my life in line, you can too, I've made
    my order.
Now it's your turn, place your order.
Are we healed, or just pretending to be? Today we laugh, tomorrow
    we're gloomy.
Happiness fleeting, like a bird in flight,
Yet in the darkness, we yearn for light.
I yearn to see that light.
A smile today, a tear tomorrow,
But somehow, I manage to hide my sorrows.
Healing isn't a straight line, it bends, of course it has unexpected
    ends.
So we question, are we really healed?
Or just in the process, our fates are still sealed.
Remember, it's okay to feel bad, but it's not okay to let it be who you
    are, you're not so bad.

*G*rowing up, I craved the feeling of love and got desperate for the attention from my mom, dad, or anyone I was around. I questioned myself, "Why doesn't anyone love me?" I thought maybe if I just did what they wanted, I would not only belong but feel loved. All I got out of it was loneliness and the longest to just let them all go and be myself for me.

Especially when I allowed fear of disappointing myself or others to take over my heart, feeling like a slave to others' expectations became suffocating. So remember, and learn from my mistakes as I say, "Don't let their desires overshadow your own. You deserve to live a life that aligns with your own dreams and aspirations."

PERFECTION

As I questioned myself, "What should I do?", should I voice it now, or keep it quiet, forget about my vow?

Life has twisted, turned, and taken flight, changing not just me, but what I thought was right.

Should I continue, let life's river flow, or wait, see them, then decide which way to go?

The truth, my truths, is mine to speak, it's my life's song to sing when the light's on me.

But I've chosen to be dependent all along.

I was never my own biggest supporter and critic every day, the saddest part, a truth I've come to know.

I've been my harshest critic every day as I allow them to bring me down each day, I'm not my own hero I'm sad to say.

Happiness eludes me, it's been a while, surrounded by darkness, struggling to smile.

And yet I kept fighting for them as they stole my smile and my pride.

Yet in the pulling, pushing, the walls closing in,

Moments of joy break through, a beacon within. But when the day ends, the question comes back, "Why doesn't anyone love me back?"

Should I voice my truth, let my feelings show, or keep them locked away, no one to know?

No, they'll get angry. I just want their love only.

Doing as they say and being quiet until I'm allowed to speak when I'm told is the only love I know.

Now let's dive into the unique challenges and experiences of being an African American woman and being a teen, from hair care to other aspects in today's society. Ready to dive in? Let's read.

GROW UP

What if he was a she,
And sitting with him was wrong, but with her, it was okay?
What if my heart fluttered for her?
Now what? Is this how it's going to be?
Rumors race as swiftly as time,
Yet you choose to squander your moments on a single lie.
A lie that many accept as truth, without questioning its origin.
Who spun this tale, where did it come from, what is its essence?
I was told no one cares about the who, the where, or the what,
At the end of the day, it's all about perspective.
But only a fool adopts another's viewpoint without verifying its accu-
    racy, that's my perspective.
I'm just a woman, but with your lie, I'm reduced to a mere nuisance.
Grow up, not just in age, but in wisdom and self-awareness.
I can admit, I haven't been as aware as I should have been, but now,
    I will be.
I know how to show compassion for all, without compromising my
    integrity.
And that's what makes me more mature, more grounded than you
    all.

I LOVE IT, EVEN THOUGH IT'S A PAIN

It's natural, but I can't take it anymore. I love my natural hair, that's for sure.

It's on me, growing to define who I am, where I'm from, it's all mine. It defines the strength, so effervescent.

Intelligence and beauty it bestows, a crown of curls, confidence it shows. Say "OH, LORD" when you relate to my journey, the love, the hate as I go. Breaking brushes, bursting headbands too, we've been there.

Spending hours to style, oh the choices we make. Crying about life's hardships, our hair is at stake.

Scared, angry, annoyed as f——k when the morning arrives. Knowing what we face, our hair, our lives.

And when someone touches without consent, we feel the invasion, our boundaries bent,

But OH, LORD, I thank you for this gift I wear. My beautiful natural hair, beyond compare.

I'm beautiful with it, it's part of me. A symbol of strength, it's all I see.

I stand tall, embracing my hair.

Thank you, my Lord, for my beautiful hair.

UNDERSTAND FOR ONCE

In a world that's already vicious, we stand strong when we act as one.
African American women, strong and majestic, we deserve all the love that's handed to us.
Our hair, always been our crown, diverse and wild, I'll keep letting it down.
In our eyes, the struggle, the joy, the pain, yet we rise, again and again.
We carry the weight, yet we soar, a pain control and yet called angry when we're at our lowest I've been told.
Unyielding spirits from our past, forever more powerful, yes, we are, from what you've been told.
In our daily struggles, we find our decree. We deserve to be loved without being in fear.

I'M A TEEN AND I'M BLACK

Being a teen isn't as easy as it seems.

Hormones coming, emotions scattering, I'm a bit scared. To make it worse, we live in a world that's quick to judge.

Our youth, a challenge, yet a gift, in a society that's often drifting. Our skin, a painting rich and bold, telling tales of the old.

Yet we're more than all the things that encounter the eye.

We horseplay, sob, we dare to dream, in a world that's not what it appears to be.

Through spars and conquests, we find our way. African American teens, we're here to stay.

UNFORGETTABLE KING, DR. MARTIN LUTHER KING

In a world where it's fight or flight, our kind fought every night.
Marching for hours for a dream that became ours.
Dr. King became everyone's knight.
His words, his hope, that dream of his made hope so strong for teens
    to stand up and fight to belong.
Because of my king, I can stand up and belong.
He teaches them to fight for what is right, to challenge injustice cause
    that's what's right.
No violence needed cause he's that man.
Because of my kind, when I'm done wrong, I'll take my stand.
Because of our king, I can dream for what's right for me.
Martin Luther King's dream was dreamt for you and me.
Because of him, I have the power to steer.
Let's forever honor his legacy in our dreams.

Embracing failure is a journey, not a destination. It's a dance with uncertainty, a tryst with the unknown. It's okay to fail, and it's okay to keep going. It's also normal to want to walk away when challenges arise. I've been there too. I've walked away from many challenges in my life, only to find myself returning, drawn back by the nagging feeling of unfinished business. I've wrestled with the discomfort of giving up, the sting of surrender. But each time, I've learned that it's not the act of walking away that defines us but the courage to return, to face our failures, and to keep going. Because in the grand scheme of life, it's not about never failing but about never stopping in our pursuit of growth and to keep going.

DO IT AGAIN

Each trial feels like a different line,
I tell myself, "I can do this," time after time.
But there are moments when I stumble and fall,
Failing starts to feel like a hobby, despite giving my all.
Behind closed doors, I'm as smart as a bee,
But in your presence, as dumb as a rock I seem to be.
The first time, it's okay, the second, I give it another try,
By the third, I'm lying to myself, saying, "At least I tried."
I've never been a quitter, but with each failure, a part of me dies,
Yet it fuels my spirit, gives me more reasons to rise.
I'm going to try, this isn't a lie.
I wish I were lying, but the pain is real,
Every effort I make, every wound I heal. But in this cycle of trials
    and falls,
I've learned to rise, to scale these walls. Because every stumble, every
    defeat,
Is just another story of the battles I beat.

I FAILED, AND THAT'S ALL RIGHT

First attempts, I always fail.
If there's a wall I will try to break.
Stumbles, tumbles, I always seem to trip and fall. But does that stop
　　me?
No, not at all.
I've failed, and that's perfectly all right. Each failure, a lesson, a step-
　　ping stone,
A path to success, uniquely my own.
First tries may falter, they may fall,
But they've never managed to stall my call. For every stumble, every
　　plight,
I rise stronger, ready to fight.
I enjoy every push and turn, I'll be all right. Each failure adds its own
　　light.
I've failed, yes, that's quite all right,
For it shaped me, made me a dynamite.

GIVE UP?

I am a warrior, raw and real.
It's normal to fail, that shit is real.
Wearing scars from battles, each a testament of zeal.
Failures, like relentless waves, crash upon my shore,
Yet ready to endure more.
The truth is harsh, it's hard to bear,
I failed again and again, I don't care.
Trials and errors, they come in heaps,
Yet my spirit, it never goes asleep.
Each stumble, each fall, part of my rhyme.
Hey, that rhyme, I love to rhyme.
Failure is daunting, never mind that, I still rise, time after time.
But say your name, and repeat it as you say, "I, I am dynamite," after
    you failed.
For in each failure, in each slip,
I find the strength, I tighten my grip. Yes, I fail, but I never bow,
For I'm a warrior, here and now.

I'm going to share a journey that's deeply personal and, at times, incredibly challenging. Yes, I still make mistakes, but I've learned to recognize when I'm going the wrong way. It's a journey of love, loss, and learning. For a long time, I found it difficult to love someone back, and if I'm being truly honest, I've never actually been able to love anyone back. A struggle that was deeply rooted in the absence of a father figure, my life made me despise being around my mom at the time. This void often led me to seek love in the wrong places, in the wrong people. Mistaking infatuation for genuine affection. I became rushed to have lust.

I've made mistakes, believed in illusions of love, and felt the deep sting of heartbreak when I got hurt. I've shed tears, hoped for change, and faced disappointment when they say they'll change. But through it all, I've learned that it's okay to keep searching, to keep hoping. Because finding the one you truly connect with, the one who understands and loves you for who you are, and what you were is worth the wait. It's a journey, not a destination, and every step, every stumble, brings us closer to finding our own version of love.

CAN I LIE

I can't keep up this lie, it's weighing me down,
Flying high like the birds, my truth needs to be found.
I yearn to soar freely, without hiding behind a facade,
But your eyes see through, my words feeling flawed.
Our desires diverge, we're on different paths,
Yet I can't help but feel this distraction, it lasts.
The beginning was sweet, but now it feels toxic,
Your smile seems fake, is it all just a trick?
I don't want to be hurt, but being with you brings pain,
I'm avoiding the truth, hoping it won't remain.
But deep down, I long to feel wanted and desired,
This feeling of being unwanted, I'm becoming tired.
It's hard to accept that we're nothing, it's true,
But facing the reality is something I must do.
I'm in denial, but slowly becoming more aware,
I need to consider the fact that we're going nowhere.

I'M HERE

In the stillness of the night,
There's a heart yearning for companionship, a melody out of tune.
Wishing for a friend, someone to share the day,
Someone to lend an ear, when words just want to play.
To the lonely hearts, I say, don't let the silence win,
For every soul has a story, waiting to begin.
A friend may seem distant, like a star in the night,
But remember, even stars are born from the absence of light.
In the quiet, in the solitude, in the moments in between,
Know that there's a world waiting to be seen.
A friend may be a message away, so don't be afraid to send a hey.
To the lonely hearts, I promise, the night will turn to day,
And you'll find a friend in an unexpected way.
So hold on to hope, let your heart be your guide,
For in the journey of loneliness, friends often coincide.
Would you like to be my friend?

ASSUME

You assumed my intentions, without a clue,
But I'm more than what you assumed to be true.
Your words hold power, they shape what you see,
Yet I longed for you to truly believe in me.
You assumed I'd bring trouble, cause only strife,
But deep down, I wanted to be a part of your life, I wish that was a
        lie.
You barely scratched the surface, barely knew,
All I wanted was a chance when I was ready too.
Yet your assumptions took hold, clouding your view,
Leaving me standing there, feeling all your blame undue.
Silent I stayed, thinking it was the best way to end,
To end the anger, the blame, and the assumptions that offend.
I don't want it to end this way, it's never too late,
To break free from assumptions, to change our fate.
I don't know what you're going through, it's true,
But I don't want to assume, I just want to be there for you.

NO MORE

No more battles, no more fights.
Yes, I'm angry, I won't lie.
I yearn for tranquility, for peace,
For a heart that's at ease.
No more longing for a touch,
No more wanting, it's too much.
To heal, to breathe, to embrace, I need that for me.
No more dreams of love so deep,
No more promises to keep.
No more tears, no more pain,
No more love's enchanting strain.
With self-love, as my guide.
I will follow that guide.
No more "us," no more "we,"
No more love, I wish to be free.
I yearn for me, to be my own.
In my heart, where I belong.
I just want to be alone.

YOU KNOW ME BETTER
THAN I KNOW *ME*

You know me better than I know myself,
You make me feel better than I've ever felt.
Every thought of you brightens my day,
Washing away any darkness that comes my way.
The way you look at me, so desirable,
A look that makes me forget anything regrettable.
I cherish every moment spent with you,
And despise every moment when we're apart, it's true.
When I sleep and dream, my thoughts reset,
But your name flows through my veins, I can't forget.
Thinking of you brings me joy, it's clear,
Knowing I'm on your mind, every second, every time.
But with feelings so strong, there's a fear,
Of getting too attached, not knowing how to let go, my dear.
Yet fate brought us together, it seems,
From the moment I slid up on Snap, sharing my dreams.
It's just the vibes we share, so strong,
When I'm mad, you understand what went wrong.
When I'm upset, you find a way to make it right,
When I'm happy, your happiness shines so bright.
When I miss you, you miss me too,
When I think of you, you appear, it's true.
It's crazy how having you on my mind,
Makes you feel the same way, an unbreakable bind.
And your touch, oh, it's something else,

Unstoppable and unbelievable, like nothing else.
Your arms around me, the best hug I've felt,
Never wanting to let go, in your embrace I melt.
The way you kiss, it's pure bliss,
A taste of love, a moment I never want to miss.

I WANT IT

What does it feel to be in love, I wonder,
Is it like the sky filled with lightning and thunder?
Or is it calm like a serene summer night?
With stars twinkling, oh what a sight.
Or is it like a mystery, deep and profound?
A feeling so vast, it's hard to sound.
What is love?
Does it make you dance, does it make you sing?
Does it make you feel like a bird on the wing?
Or does it make you quiet, thoughtful, and still?
A feeling so deep, it's hard to fill.
I yearn to know, to understand,
To hold love's essence in my hand.
To feel its warmth, to know its grace,
To see its reflection in my face.
I want to know what it feels to be in love,
Is it as gentle as the cooing of a dove?
I want to feel love.
A feeling so powerful, it sets you free.
So here I stand, heart open wide,
Ready for love's mysterious ride.
Yearning to know, to feel, to see,
What it truly feels, to be in love, to be free.

MEMORIZE

In the intensity of loss, I yearn to speak,
But my words to you are nothing more than whispers in the wind,
      listen to me.
Conversing with you is like grappling with amnesia,
Best to remember, for later it will be a weapon in your arsenal.
Trying to align with you, but being with you feels like a puzzle in
      my room,
Spaced out, confused, overwhelmed, yet beneath it all, a sense of
      calm persists.
I glance at you, sensing you're not with your heart's desire,
Ironically, that's exactly how I feel.
"It will be alright, I've got you, I love you."
But is it really all right? Do you truly love me?
If I question my love for you,
Does it mean my love is wavering?
My thoughts, like a relentless tide, drain me,
Why can't I do anything right?
Why can't I say anything right?
The exhaustion of incessant self-doubt is overwhelming,
Proving my love for you day after day, only to realize I'm questioning
      it.
Our relationship, like a hiccup, sporadic and unpredictable,
Neither of us is blind to the delusion, what we want to be right isn't.
You label us as lust, but I yearn for love,
You're strong, straight, real with me,
Yet I'm weak, curved, questioning my authenticity with you.
I find myself transforming day by day for you,

Because being myself seems to be a nuisance to you.
Memorize, oh memorize, the conversation I yearn to have,
Memorize the responses I would give,
Memorize your daily moods, I'm tired of this.

DIFFERENT

This time is different, unexpected in its own way,
We both had walls, tall and strong, but different in what they convey.
Yours, built of rock, mine, made of stone,
But neither of us wanted to feel alone.
You sought love, while I craved something more,
My walls stood firm, but love wasn't what they were for.
Yet I kept building, hoping the absence of pain,
Would dull the hurt, never to be felt again.
But why, oh why, is this pain still here?
If I've convinced myself, your absence no longer exists.
The way you speak, I respected, but didn't adore,
And how you saw me, I couldn't fully explore.
Imagining life without you, it's hard to conceive,
Though I know deep down, I can still live and achieve.
I've endured hurt and lies, but the ultimate blow,
Was when you became a lie, a truth I couldn't show.
Why did things have to stay the same,
When we both desired a change, a different game?
In the end, what set us apart, so clear,
You made me feel like an option, while you were my dear.
That's what makes us different, my lover,
You were a choice, while I made you my priority, till the end.

REPLACE

It's so quiet, I could almost hear my thoughts
With all your personalities, I can barely figure out which one I'm
      talking to Most days.
Without a doubt, someone ends up running out
I wished you had turned around
But pride had won
And here I go again
Yes, I remember I ran out too, I let my pride take over.
Only ended up hurting myself by the day,
I didn't get to apologize,
What am I saying?
I hated the thought of a goodbye.
You have already erased me, I needed you. BYE!

I'M BUGGIN'

I might have set myself up for failure.
All wound up in my feelings, a familiar tale.
Remember the saying, "Best night I'll never forget,"
But alas, it seems I've let it slip.
Trying to piece together a puzzle with no pieces,
Each attempt, the wrong size, the confusion increases.
Words that blur yet feel so deep,
Meaning something to me yet lost in sleep.
How can I remember what seems to be lost?
Why does it feel like I'm paying the cost?
I'm starting to feel I'm the worst,
Did I utter something, a bubble burst?
I remember the way he held me tight,
The way he kissed me that night.
That memory lingers, refusing to go,
Fear creeps in, but I don't want to let go.
Feelings stir, they've taken control,
I'm bugging, caught in an emotional toll.
Pushing him away, though he's already far,
It's a cruel game, love's bizarre.
For once, I want someone to fear losing me as I feel Scotter
Guess I'm just better off being free.
It's painful to realize, we laugh together, dine,
Yet in our solitary moments, we cry alone.

NO LABEL

Your kisses, like soft whispers, trace from my lips,
Caressing slowly, moving toward my tender breast. "I like that,"
I whisper, as desire ignites within.
My hands entangled in your hair, gently caressing, while I kiss his
    lips.
Let me kiss your neck, feeling your pulse quicken.
Do you like that?
Your gaze says it all.
"Stop that," I say teasingly with a playful smile,
Because I like that.
Your eyes locked on mine.
No words can capture the intensity of this feeling,
What is that?
A touch that sets my soul ablaze.
It's not love, it's a passionate connection.
I didn't like that.
Yet, we tread on dangerous ground, without labels,
Asking for trouble, but wait, don't stop now.
I like the way you handle me, come on top of me,
Yes, like that, let our desires intertwine.
But too much lust can consume us, overwhelm us,
Compassion without passion, I'll pass.
Yet I can't forget the memory of your touch.
You're in too deep, and I like that, can't you see?
But I know you're not like that, so what is this?
Perhaps we should stop, but right now, all I want is that,
Or is it just the intensity of the moment that I'm feeling?

Why'd you stop? I don't like that.
Kiss me again, yes, just like that,
And don't you dare stop, I like that.

I APOLOGIZE

I apologize for feeling like I'm always in third place,
I've let you hurt me twice, and it's hard to erase.
The second time, I blame myself for letting it occur,
It's always something or work, making me feel unsure.
I've begged for you to make an effort, to do something more,
But even a walk in the park feels like a closed door.
I long to see you outside of your confined space,
To feel your kiss in a world beyond your room's embrace.
You expect communication, but why am I the last to know?
Is this how you envision our love will continue to grow?
It's not just about being seen, it's about feeling it's real,
But now I've grown silent, and your anger I can feel.
Don't use the excuse of being busy, I see through the lies,
Knowing I'll never be a priority, it's hard to disguise.
I can be around you, enjoying your company and presence,
But it's like I don't feel you, creating a sense of distance.
I can barely be myself around you, it's always been this way,
You get mad if I express my feelings, causing dismay.
You find me annoying when I speak up or act strange when I'm quiet,
We're both messing things up, our connection feels unquiet.
Leaving little energy to give, making it hard for us to withstand.
I'm tired of not knowing how to reach you when I'm feeling low,
When I'm ready to explode, afraid to let my emotions show.
I just want to be seen outside of your room's walls,
To be able to express my emotions without causing falls.
I want our love to be more than just a physical presence,
To feel connected emotionally, creating a deeper essence.

IT'S DIFFERENT

Turning our backs, neither here nor there,
Fault lines blur, losing myself in despair.
Never enough, we both fall short,
Seeing each other as a last resort.
Different desires, same goals in sight,
Different paths, in the same plight.
Life's a game, with an uncertain end,
A tie, a win, or just pretend?
Will we reconcile, put differences aside,
Or let the game of life divide?
Now, I'm in line, waiting in vain,
For words that might ease the pain.
He's into her, I'm supposed to be fine,
My voice drowned, in the silent brine.
Should I move on, I question my heart,
He's the "it," tearing me apart.
"I'm your choice," I yearn to say,
But he's chosen her, I'm led astray.
His attention, his words, all for her,
I'm invisible, a silent observer.
Hurt resurfaces, emotions overflow,
We promised honesty, but what does he show?
Walking aimlessly, sun blinding my sight,
Confusion reigns, day feels like night.
Writing this down, a cathartic release,
A moment's respite, a fleeting peace.

IS HE MR. RIGHT?

Just met a boy, I call him White,
His presence alone makes everything bright.
The way he smiles makes me feel so light
I like him more as he spends the night
His laughter, a melody, that's soft but loud sometimes it's funny the
      way he frowns
When he's gone I think of him.
Our conversations, like a gentle stream,
A connection so instant, it feels like a dream.
I hope he never leaves
I like him, oh, more than I can say,
In his company, I wish to stay.
The bond between us, growing each day,
I hope it never fades away.
But if it does I know for a fact I'll feel doomed.
In his world, I found a place for me.
With every shared laugh, every whispered word,
A symphony of feelings within me stirred.
I hope this bond, so beautiful and rare,
Stays with us, like a breath of fresh air.

THE TRUTH

I understand that you're feeling conflicted
and unsure about what to do.
It's not easy when life takes unexpected turns and
you're faced with important decisions. It's natural to
question and doubt ourselves in these moments.
Being independent can be empowering, but it also means being
your own supporter and critic. It's important to acknowledge
that you haven't always been supportive of yourself in the right
way. Remember, it's never too late to start being kind and
supportive to yourself, especially when facing challenges.
Feeling unhappy and suffocated is tough, but it's
encouraging that you have moments of happiness that
break through the negativity. Find your moments.
As for what you should do, I can't make that decision for you.
However, I encourage you to listen to your intuition, trust yourself,
and consider what will bring you true happiness and fulfillment.
Sometimes, taking a leap of faith and speaking your truth can
lead to incredible growth and positive changes. You deserve to
be heard and to live a life that aligns with your authentic self.

Don't let the mistake you've made because of your past
have done to you determine who you are now.

I'm ready to embrace the day, my past fears are gone.
I am not what I was, I can choose to be what I want.
In the mirror of my dreams, my future, I see.
No more scarred glass, I'm happy.

I'm growing, and evolving finally
In the forest of existence, finding my own height.
I want to live, to laugh, to learn, to explore,
To taste the sweetness of life, like never before.
In the journey of self-discovery, I find my way,
In the silence of my heart, I hear it say,
"To love, to be loved, is the greatest quest,
In my book of life, it's the loveliest jest."
So here I am, ready to unfurl, to grow, to love, to be free and wild.
Stepping into tomorrow, with a hopeful heart,
Ready to play my own, unique part.
I am the artist, and life is my canvas,
With every brushstroke, I find my purpose.
I'm not just surviving, but truly living.
In the quest for love, I find my one, no more rush I'm done.
I am the artist, my life is the clay,
Molding my destiny, in my unique way.
I've learned to dance in the rain, to embrace the storm,
To see beauty in change, in every form.
I've found that love is not just about another's touch,
But about loving myself, just as much.
Cheers to me, I can say, "I love myself just as much today."
In the story of life, I'm the hero, the lead,
Growing, loving, living—that's my creed.

Here's a suggestion to you all.

As we reach the end of this chapter of my life, I want to express my deepest gratitude to you, the reader. Your time and presence throughout this journey have been invaluable.

This book has been a testament to transformation, the power of self-reflection, and growth of myself. Yes, I am still a work in progress, and there's beauty in that. I'm not rushing into any relationships but taking my time to understand myself better.

My past, filled with its trials and tribulations, has shaped me into the person I am today—and for that, I am grateful. I am happier, stronger, and more in tune with myself.

I hope my journey inspires you to embrace your past, to see it not as a series of failures but as stepping stones toward becoming a better version of yourself. Remember, it's okay to take your time. It's okay to be a work in progress.

Thank you for being a part of my story. Here's to our continued journey toward self-discovery and happiness with me.

Like Akon said, "The life you have is borrowed. You're not promised tomorrow, so live your life as if it's your last." So when will you let your wounds heal?

Would you like to tell me your story?

____

____

____

____

____

____

____

____

____

ABOUT THE AUTHOR

Ycarp Leahcimrac was born in Guyana and grew up in the United States, in New York City. Leahcimrac's journey has been a winding path, filled with complex emotions and tough lesson, mostly being raised in a Caribbean household. She has always kept her friend group small but knew everyone. Growing up, she has always been a daddy's little girl, yet family dynamics often felt like a puzzle with pieces that didn't quite fit. The people who were supposed to be her protectors sometimes turned into the very tempests, whom she needed shelter from. Yes, they made her felt unloved and unworthy, but she didn't let that define her. Leahcimrac found interest in poetry in the ending of middle school. When she started to write, it was never the best, but she knew what she meant. Pursuing to become a writer, Leachcimrac didn't stop in high school. It has always been a struggle for her to speak her mind, and that's when the decision to hunt for the best publisher came to mind. *2004* is her first poetry book, and she doesn't plan to stop there. As she embraces her story, each day, she writes a new page, hoping to inspire others with her perseverance.

www.ingramcontent.com/pod-product-compliance
Lightning Source LLC
Chambersburg PA
CBHW022115150726
47990CB00003B/1352